Y0-DLD-728

001.64
B   Bitter, Gary G.

C1   Exploring with
           computers

DATE DUE

LEWIS SCHOOL LIBRARY
1431 N. LEAMINGTON AVE.
CHICAGO, ILLINOIS 60651

# EXPLORING WITH COMPUTERS

EXPLORING WITH COMPUTERS

GARY G. BITTER

Illustrated with Photographs

LEWIS SCHOOL LIBRARY
1431 N. LEAMINGTON AVE.
CHICAGO, ILLINOIS 60651

JULIAN MESSNER
NEW YORK

Copyright © 1981, 1983 by Gary G. Bitter

All rights reserved including the right of
reproduction in whole or in part in any form.
Published by Julian Messner,
Division of Simon & Schuster, Inc.
Simon & Schuster Building,
1230 Avenue of the Americas,
New York, New York 10020.
JULIAN MESSNER and colophon are trademarks of
Simon & Schuster, Inc.

10 9 8 7 6 5 4 3 2 1
10 9 8 7 6 5 4 3 2 1 Pbk.

Manufactured in the United States of America

Library of Congress Cataloging in Publication Data

Bitter, Gary G.
   Exploring with computers.

  Includes index.
  Summary: Discusses how computers work, their types, uses, misuses, computers of the future, and careers in the field. Includes computer-related activities.
   1. Computers—Juvenile literature. 2. Electronic data processing—Juvenile literature. [1. Computers] I. Title.
QA76.23.B55   1983   001.64   83-7917
ISBN 0-671-47789-7

ISBN 0-671-49884-3 Pbk.

ACKNOWLEDGMENTS

Thanks to a great editor and friend, Mady Anderson, and to Linda Kay Oiler for her help in the preparation of this revised edition.

MESSNER BOOKS BY GARY G. BITTER

EXPLORING WITH COMPUTERS
EXPLORING WITH SOLAR ENERGY
(*With Thomas H. Metos*)

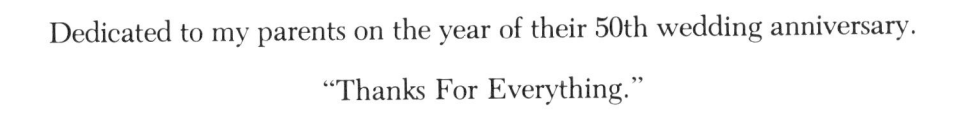

Dedicated to my parents on the year of their 50th wedding anniversary.

"Thanks For Everything."

PICTURE CREDITS

Apple Corp., p. 42-43
Atari, p. 49 top
Chrysler Corp., pp. 51, 52
Commodore Business Machines, pp. 46, 79
Epcot Center, p. 61
Hewlett-Packard Co., p. 38
IBM, pp. 10, 26, 31
Motorola, pp. 23, 24, 25, 27
New York Public Library, pp. 13, 14, 15, 17, 19, 20
Radio Shack, pp. 32, 47, 55, 59
Texas Instruments, p. 48
Wang, p. 35

Contents

What Is a Computer?	11
Computers of the Past	12
How a Computer Works	28
Hardware and Software	40
Types of Computers	44
Uses of Computers	50
Misuses of Computers	56
Computer Careers	57
Computers in the Future	60
Computer-Related Activities for You	62
Glossary	83
Index	91

A computer system.

What Is a Computer?

Science fiction stories on television, in the movies, and in books have led many people to believe that computers have mysterious powers. Some stories have even shown computers controlling the universe. These fictional computers are usually robotlike heroes or villains who can talk, walk, and think, save or destroy worlds.

But the truth about computers is that they are only machines—tools for human beings to use like you use pencils or pieces of chalk. And, just like a pencil or a piece of chalk, a computer can only do what it is directed to do by human beings. A computer's great value is that it can save human beings vast amounts of time. It can process information millions of times more rapidly than human beings can. And computers can store a tremendous amount of information for future use.

Computers of the Past

In early times, people counted on their fingers and toes—as long as there were no more than twenty objects to be counted. For counting larger quantities people used stones, pebbles, and lines drawn on the ground. Shepherds, for instance, kept a stone for each sheep in their flock. At the end of the day, they matched stones against sheep. A leftover stone meant that a sheep had wandered off or been left behind without the shepherd noticing.

When people found that using stones or drawing lines on the ground was not practical for counting or remembering large amounts, more sophisticated systems developed over many centuries. The *abacus*, an instrument used for recording numbers by sliding counters along rods or grooves within a frame, was invented. The early Romans, the Japanese, and the Chinese used different versions of the abacus.

As time went on, number systems were developed for computing figures. The Romans used signs or letters for each number. I was the letter symbol for one, V for five,

The Japanese abacus.

X for ten, L for fifty, C for 100, and D for 500. In the twelfth century, the Hindu-Arabic System used the digits 0 through 9 to represent any number, depending on the placement of the digit. This was one of the first *place-value number systems*, and it is the system we use today.

One of the earliest calculating machines using digits was invented in 1642 by Blaise Pascal, a French mathematician. About fifty of these digital calculators were built. The machine was about the size of a milk carton and had a series of wheels that were turned with a pointer to add *or* subtract. It could not do both. Pascal's machine was similar to the odometer in today's automobiles, which adds the number of miles the car travels.

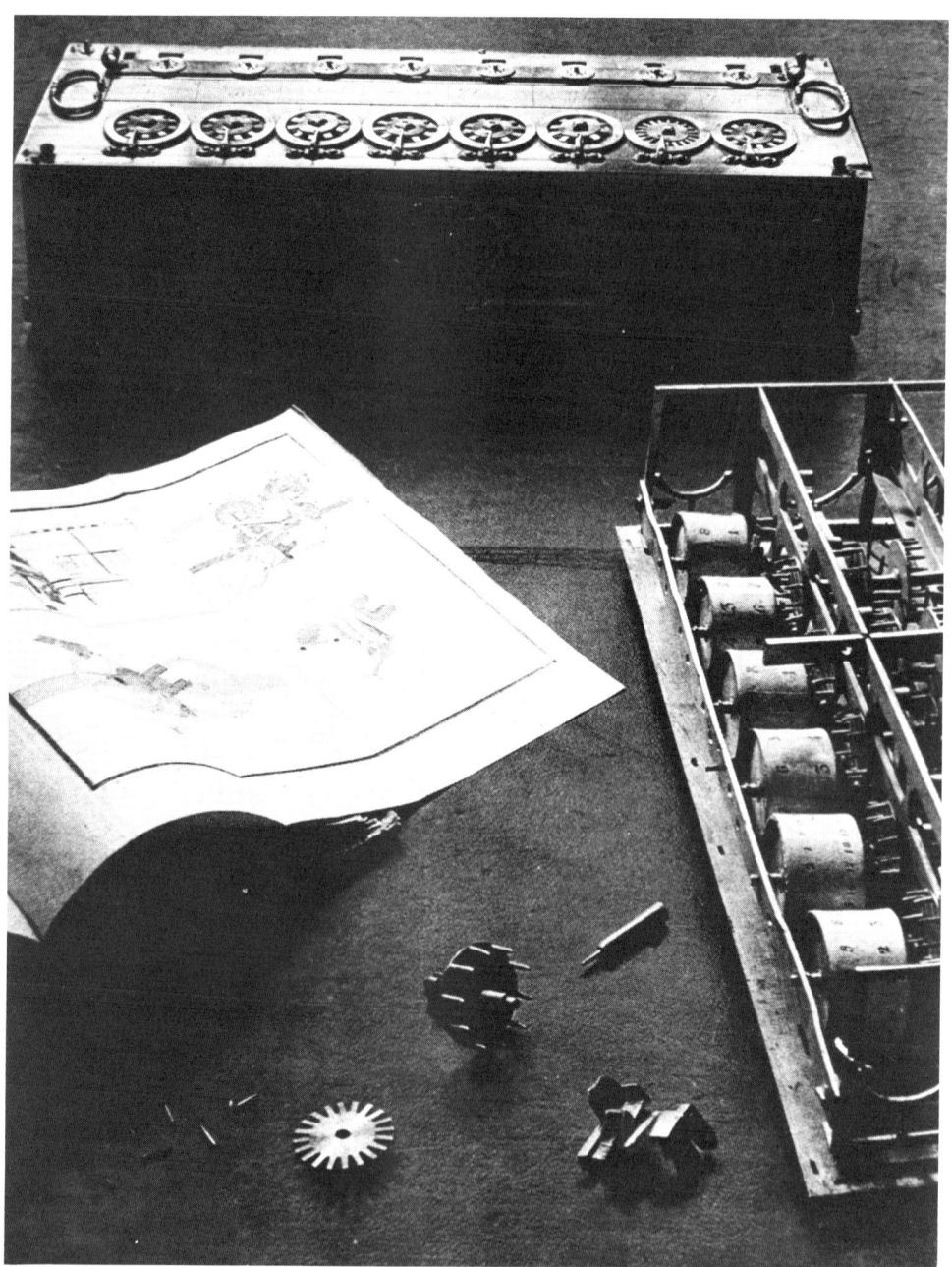
Blaise Pascal's invention was one of the earliest calculating machines.

In 1662, Samuel Morland produced another early mechanical calculator. This calculator was used to compute taxes for the nation of France. Morland's machine could add *and* subtract. To add, the wheels of the machine were turned clockwise. To subtract, the wheels were turned counter-clockwise.

A German, Gottfried Wilhelm von Leibniz, invented a calculator in 1694 that could multiply and divide as well as add and subtract. Very expensive and complicated, only two of Leibniz's calculators were ever built.

Leibniz's "reckoning machine."

15

In 1833, an Englishman named Charles Babbage proposed to build a complicated machine he called an "analytical engine." The machine was designed to solve mathematical problems at high speed, to print out the answers, and to remember them as well. But the analytical engine was never completed because its cost was too high. Several models have now been built from Babbage's detailed drawings to prove that his theories would have worked. Over a century ago, Babbage understood most of the fundamentals involved in modern-day digital computers.

Babbage was assisted in his efforts by Lady Lovelace, Augusta Ada Byron. The daughter of the great English poet Lord Byron, Lady Lovelace was a brilliant mathematician. She understood Babbage's theories and wrote the best description we now have of Babbage's proposed analytical engine. For her contributions, she has been honored by having a computer language, ADA, named after her.

Charles Babbage used cards punched in certain places to store numbers in his analytical engine. These cards were not invented by Babbage, however. J. M. Jacquard had designed a system using punched cards to control the patterns woven into cloth. In America, punched cards were first used to feed instructions to a computing machine in 1887 by Dr. Herman Hollerith. Dr. Hollerith's cards were used to process the United States census in 1890. The punched cards saved a great deal of time in taking and reporting the results of the census.

Babbage's "Analytical Engine" was finally built.

In 1937, Howard Aiken of Harvard University outlined a plan for a digital computer using relays and punched paper tape. He designed the computer to solve the difficult problems that he had encountered in his research.

In 1944, a team of engineers financed by International Business Machines (IBM) built the MARK I computer. The MARK I is considered the beginning of the modern computer era. The MARK I was a very large machine. It had more than 700,000 moving parts and used more than 500 miles of electrical wire. Computations were performed by *electro-mechanical switches*, switches physically moved by electrical currents. The MARK I could add three eight-digit numbers (like 99,999,999 and 88,888,888 and 77,777,777) in just one second. All of a computer's work is done by adding and subtracting, so the more sums they can do each second, the better.

John Vincent Atanasoff, with the help of his graduate student Clifford Berry, built a computer in 1939. A working model of the ATANASOFF-BERRY computer was completed in 1942. But it wasn't until the middle 1970s that their work became known. Today Atanasoff is acknowledged as one of the fathers of the digital computer.

Between 1943 and 1946, John William Mauchly and John Presper Eckert led a project that developed a computer called the Electronic Numerical Integrator and Computer (ENIAC). ENIAC used *vacuum tubes*, gas-filled glass tubes. This was the first completely electronic automatic computer, and it had more than 18,000 vacuum tubes and weighed about 30 tons—60,000 pounds. The ENIAC could perform about 5,000 additions per second.

Computers that used vacuum-tube technology were developed between 1945 and 1959 and are often referred to as *first-generation computers*. Vacuum tubes hold a part of the electrical patterns by which computers work. Each tube is like a piece of a jigsaw puzzle. These early computers could do about 40,000 additions per second.

ENIAC at the University of Pennsylvania became operational in 1945.

How many additions can you do in one second? Of course, when you think about how much faster a computer can add, you should also remember that there are many things that you can do that a computer cannot. But are you beginning to see how much time a computer can save? Are you beginning to see how valuable computers can be?

Vacuum tube panel.

John von Neumann, a Hungarian who became an American citizen and later served as a member of the Atomic Energy Commission, is credited with first using binary arithmetic for developing high-speed computers. *Binary arithmetic* uses only the digits 0 and 1 to represent all numbers. For computer use, therefore, a light or a magnetic or electric charge that can be turned on and off can represent the two digits. No light or charge represents the digit 0. The light or charge going on represents the digit 1. Thus an infinite number of computations are reduced to on-off simplicity. Can you see how the binary system speeds up computation?

Von Neumann also helped to design the Electronic Discrete Variable Automatic Computer (EDVAC). EDVAC was the first computer to store—or remember—a set of directions. These stored directions enabled the computer to change variables—apply new information—as it computed solutions to problems. Human beings no longer had to intervene to tell the computer to do something different when circumstances changed. This allowed computers to become even faster than they had been in the past.

The UNIVAC I (Universal Automatic Computer), developed in 1951, was the first computer to be sold to businesses. Forty-six UNIVAC I computers were delivered between 1951 and 1958.

In 1958, *transistors*, also referred to as *solid state amplifiers*, replaced vacuum tubes in computers. These transistorized or solid state computers are called *second-generation computers*. Transistors, much smaller than tubes, meant that computers could be built that were smaller and less expensive. They were also faster—they could do about 200,000 additions per second. And transistors required less electricity, produced less heat, and lasted much longer than did vacuum tubes.

Transistors were used in computers until 1964 when *integrated circuitry* or *microelectronics* was introduced.

A panel of transistors used in second-generation computers (1945-1959).

Sets of transistors in a computer could now be made in almost microscopic size, and then placed in one small single unit called an *integrated circuit*. These were third-generation computers and could do about 1,250,000 additions per second.

You can see that each generation of computers grows smaller and considerably faster than the generation before it.

The first integrated circuit, invented by Jack Kilby in 1958. This photo has been magnified many times so it looks rather primitive. Actually, the circuit holds many switches and transistors in a space of less than one-half inch.

Today we are able to mold several hundred thousand circuits into one unit, called a *chip*. A chip is about the size of a pencil eraser. This is *Large Scale Integration* (LSI), because while the integrated circuits are smaller, more of them can be packed into a chip. LSI became available in the early 1970s.

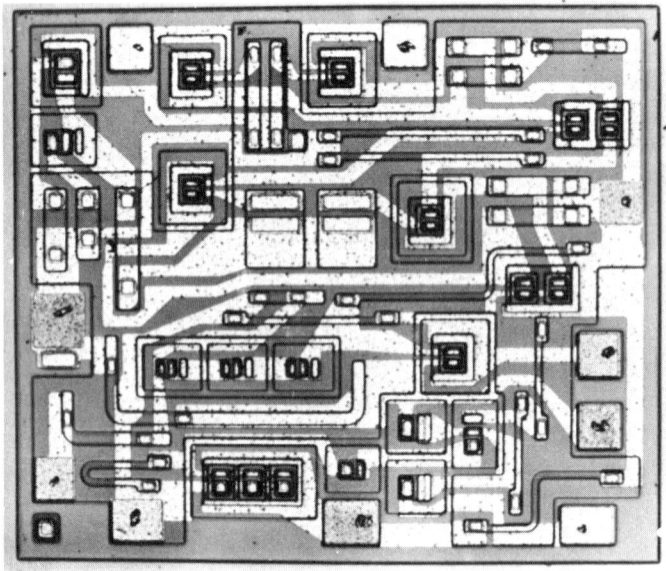

An integrated circuit dated 1974.

In 1975, *Very Large Scale Integration* (VLSI) improved Large Scale Integration, making computers still smaller and less expensive. Today's computers, generally thought of as *fourth-generation computers*, perform millions of additions per second.

Chips are constantly becoming smaller and smaller and, at the same time, can include more and more

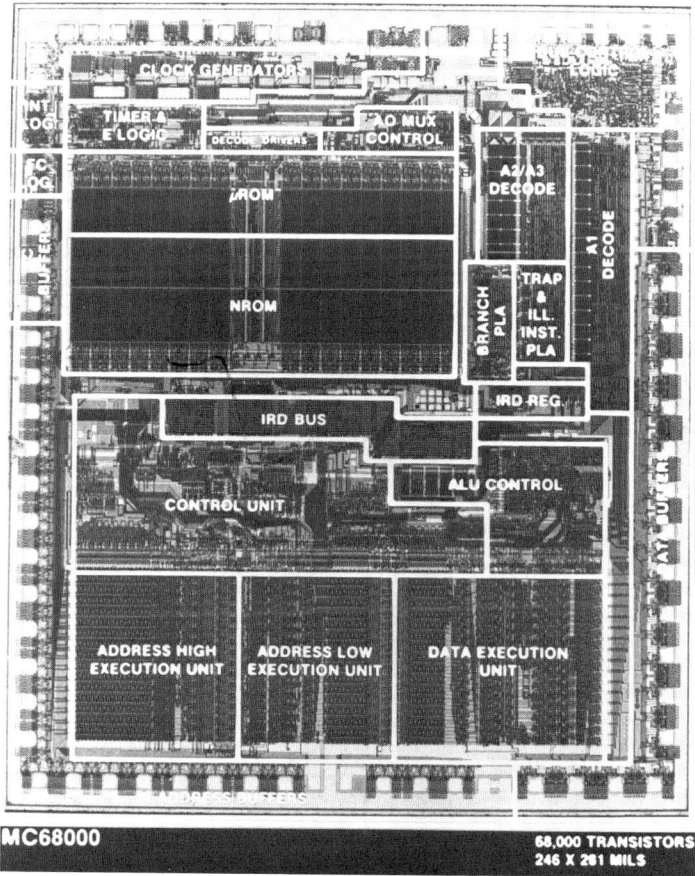

Chip transistors used in third-generation computers.

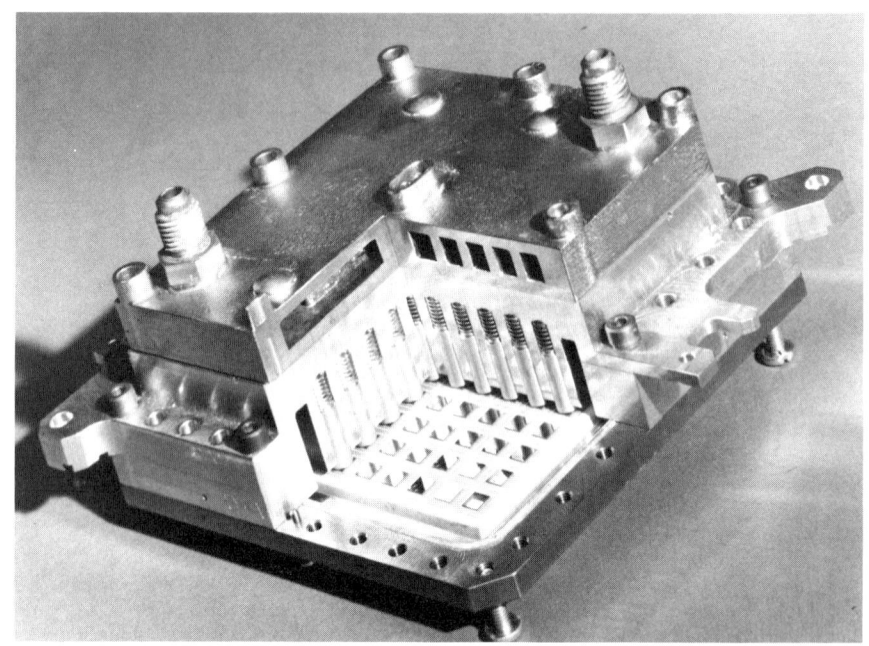

This is a cut-away photo of an IBM module made up of 118 chips, introduced in 1981.

computer components. The workings of most early digital computers, some as large as a living room, could be put into one present-day chip the size of a penny!

Fourth-generation computers have already been developed that can add or subtract more than *one billion* times per second! These computers are used to keep track of the enormous amounts of data sent back to the earth from orbiting satellites. The Hewlett-Packard Corporation has designed a computer chip with a 450,000-

transistor capacity. In a single second, this computer can process and record the information contained in 1,000 books to contain.

What do you think the fifth-generation computers will be able to do? Many computer experts predict that artificial intelligence will be created in computers so that they will function without human control.

This is the M6800 single-chip computer, photographed on top of a dime to show the amazingly small size of the new microprocessors.

27

How a Computer Works

When you are asked to multiply the numbers 6 and 5, you need your ears to hear the problem or your eyes to see it, your mouth to speak the answer or your hand to write it, and one part of your brain to remember the numbers. You also need a part of the brain to multiply the numbers and another part of the brain to control all of these activities. A computer works the same way.

Human	*Problem*	*Computer*
Touch, hear or see	Numbers 6 and 5	Input — data cards — cathode ray tube — terminal
Coordinate in your brain	Coordinate the activity	Central Processing Unit
Remember in your brain	Remember 6 and 5	Memory
Compute in your brain	Multiply	Arithmetic Unit
Voice or touch	Give answer 30	Output — cathode ray tube — hard-copy printer

Input, memory, central processing unit, arithmetic unit, and output are the main parts that make up a computer.

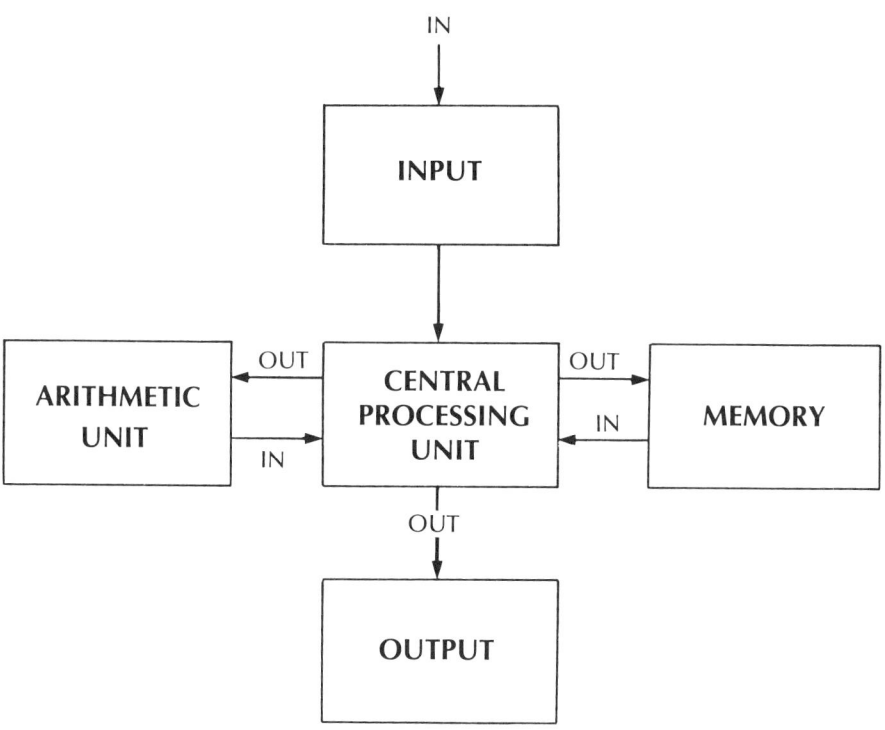

Input

Input is *information*—either in the form of program instructions, or in the form of data to be processed. The most common way of entering input into the computer is through a *computer terminal*. A computer terminal has a keyboard like a typewriter. We give our instructions and data, our information, to the computer by typing on the terminal. As we type, our input appears on a television-like screen called a *Cathode Ray Tube* (CRT). Or the information appears on paper printers, usually called *hard-copy terminals* or *teletypewriters*.

Although it is becoming less popular than other methods, another way to send information to the computer is by *punch* or *data cards*. Information is coded on the cards using a machine called a *keypunch*. The keypunch uses the specific code that the computer has been designed to work with. The punched cards go through a special machine called a *card reader* that sorts the cards and sends the information to the proper place in the computer.

Still another method of input is a special light device that reads coding. You see this coding as a series of lines and numbers printed on things you buy. The coded information is sent by the light device to the computer. The next time you are shopping in a department store or supermarket, see if this code is used to send the cost of your purchase to a computer.

A keypunch machine used to record information on data cards.

31

Central Processing Unit

The *Central Processing Unit* (CPU) is the computer's control center, its "brain." The CPU is made up of the *Control Unit* and the *Arithmetic/Logic Unit*. The CPU receives, sorts, and distributes all information, sending and receiving from the Arithmetic Unit, Memory, Input, and Output. Information sent to Output is in a form readable by the computer user.

This hard-copy terminal used for input and output is small enough to fit in a pocket.

Arithmetic/Logic Unit

The arithmetic/logic unit is part of the CPU and controlled by the CPU. It performs all necessary computations. The human brain also has a specific region for doing computations. But in a computer these computations are done at a much faster rate of speed.

Memory

In a computer there are two basic types of memory: *primary* and *secondary*. Primary memory is storage space that is contained inside the computer. Secondary memory is storage space that is outside the computer.

Primary Storage

Computer storage space is measured in amounts represented by the letter K, meaning kilobyte. A *kilobyte* is the space required to store 1,024 numbers, letters, or punctuation marks. For example, a computer with a memory of 16K can store 16,384 (16 × 1,024) numbers, letters, or punctuation marks at one time. The larger the K number, the greater the capability of the computer to compute as well as to store information.

Today, the memory of a computer is mainly *semiconductor memory*. Electronic semiconductors are small, inexpensive, and very reliable. *Read Only Memory* (ROM) is a common type of semiconductor memory. ROM is built into the computer when the computer is manufactured. ROM instructions and information cannot be changed by the user. *Random Access Memory* (RAM) is also a form of semiconductor memory, but one that can be changed by the user at any time. Programs written to solve a particular problem are usually stored in RAM. Once the problem is worked through and the computer is turned off, the RAM memory is lost unless it has been transferred to secondary memory storage.

In addition to semiconductor memory, primary storage may be *magnetic core memory*. A magnetic core is made up of many metal rings shaped like doughnuts, so small that many would fit on the head of a pin. Information is stored by the direction of magnetic charges at each wire crossing in the doughnut.

Closeup of a magnetic core.

Secondary Storage

We human beings can store a certain amount of information in our brains. But we also use books, tape recordings, phonograph records, and film to store information. The computer does not have a brain like ours, but it does have secondary storage devices like tapes and records to hold information until the CPU needs it. Two popular forms of secondary storage are *magnetic tape* and *magnetic disk*, similar to the cassette tapes and records we are used to playing on our stereos. Many small home computers use tapes or disks to store information.

Magnetic disk used to store computer information.

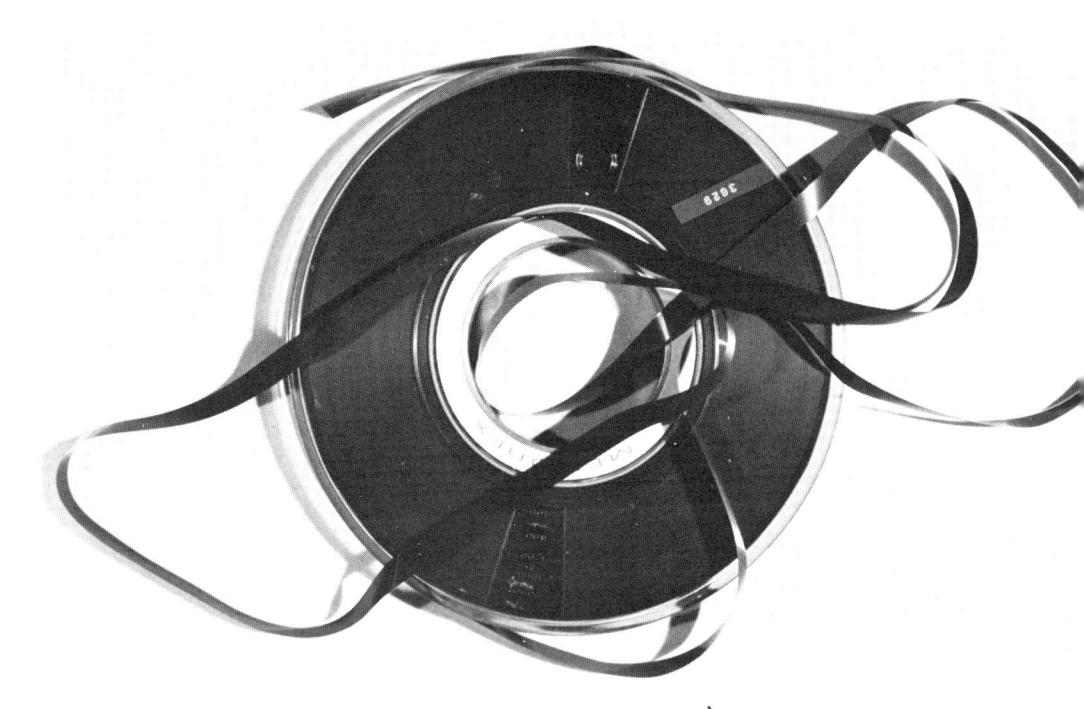

Magnetic tape used to store computer information.

Output

Output is the information that the computer has come up with, or the answers to the problems you have given as input. The hard-copy terminal, or teletypewriter, is the most common method of giving output.

If printed copies of information are not needed, the output is usually displayed on a CRT. Many banks use CRTs to find out the status of a client's accounts. Bankers only need to refer to the data once, perhaps to approve a check or to verify a transaction. They do not need printed copies to refer to later. You might also see a CRT at passenger check-in counters at airports. These are used to confirm your airline reservations and to give you your seat assignment.

This CRT is used to send and receive information.

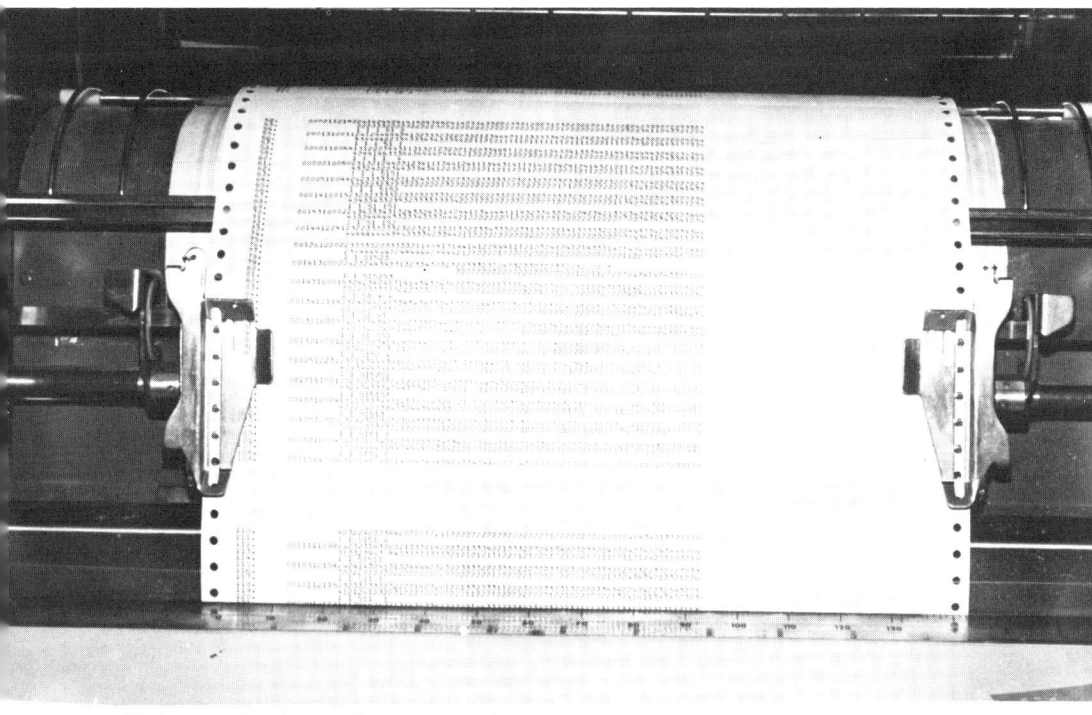

A high-speed printer of computer data.

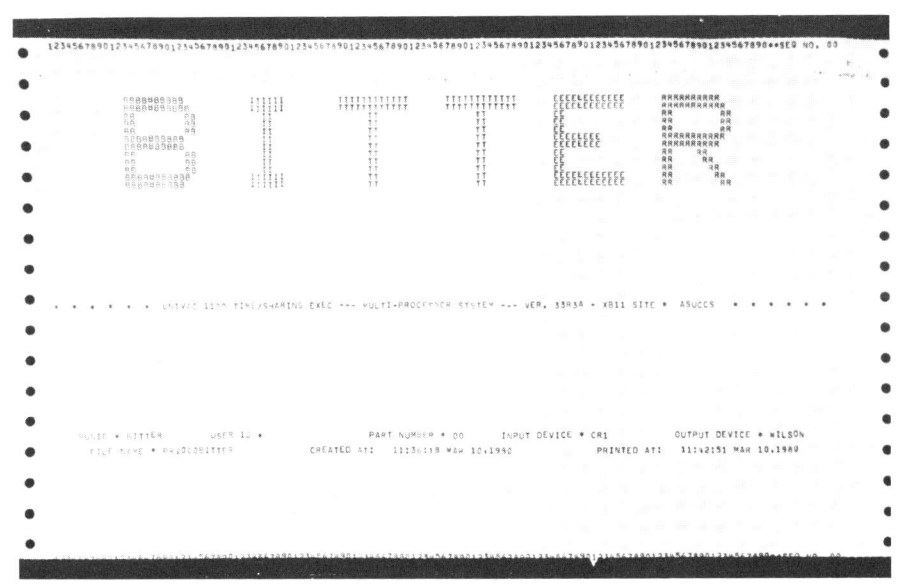

The first page of output from a computer.

Hardware and Software

Computer *hardware* and *software* are common terms used when talking about computers.

Software refers to the set of instructions or programs given to the computer. There are two types of software: 1) applications software, and 2) systems software.

Applications software is written to tell the computer how to solve a particular problem. For instance, applications software may tell the computer how to calculate the average test results of a class.

Systems software helps to control and schedule the parts of the computer system, and tells the computer operator what the computer is doing. Computers cannot function without systems software.

There are many special software languages that help human beings to communicate with computers. Some of them are BASIC, FORTRAN, COBOL, LOGO, Forth, and Pascal. Just as there are different languages spoken in many countries around the world, there are also different computer languages for different uses. FORTRAN is often used by scientists and engineers while COBOL is most often used in businesses. LOGO is used in many elementary schools. Most computers can work in several different languages.

Hardware is the equipment that makes up a computer system. Disks, CPUs, printers, and CRTs are all computer hardware.

Hardware—a printer of computer data.

A small computer system with two disk drives, a CRT, a printer, and a phone.

43

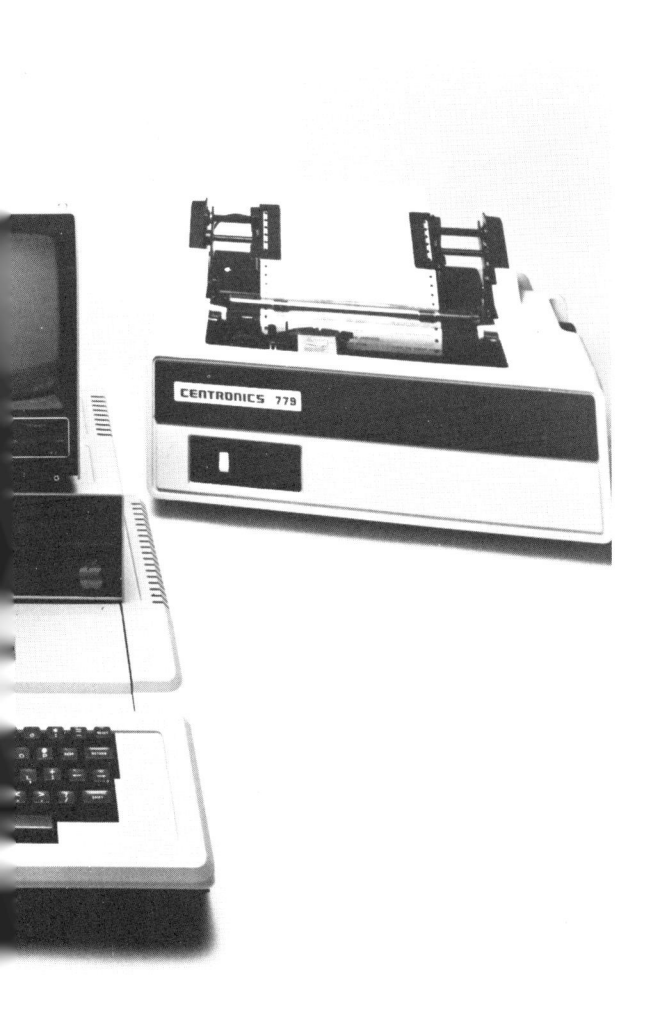

Types of Computers

There are many different types of computers. The largest are *mainframe computer systems*. The U.S. Department of Defense uses a mainframe computer system to keep track of military operations. Banks use these computer systems to keep track of vast financial dealings. Hundreds of other industries with large amounts of information to process also use mainframe computer systems.

Minicomputer systems have many of the same features that mainframe systems have. However, they have less storage capacity. Minicomputers are medium-sized computer systems. Minicomputers are less expensive and, therefore, are used widely in businesses and schools for bookkeeping, inventory, and other record-keeping.

Time-sharing allows many users to share a computer at the same time. A terminal and telephone are used to gain access to the computer. For example, a person in Phoenix, Arizona, can use a computer in New York City if he or she has a terminal, telephone number, and computer code for identification. In this manner, many users share the cost of a system that they could not afford to purchase themselves.

A time-sharing computer system. It can service up to 128 work stations like these six.

A portable terminal using a telephone.

A very popular computer is the *microcomputer* or *home computer*. Some of these systems can be purchased for less than $100. Many microcomputers have color displays, and some can reproduce sounds similar to the human voice. The home computer has many uses. It can be used for keeping household records, teaching various skills, and even for playing games and providing entertainment. Small businesses use microcomputers for inventory, financial information, and general records. Schools use them to solve problems and to teach various

The wide use of computers in business assures many career opportunities in the computer field.

The Texas Instruments TI 99/4 home computer.

Computers can teach many different skills.

And they can also be used to play games like checkers.

subjects. One of the most useful applications of a microcomputer is training through simulations, creating conditions similar to real experiences.

Microprocessors are computer chips that can be programmed to operate various things. These are presently used to operate microwave ovens, ignition systems in cars, television sets, and many other appliances and technical equipment. Most electronic games are controlled by microprocessors.

Uses of Computers

Computers are used in almost every profession and industry. Banks and stock brokerage houses use computers to keep records of customers' accounts as well as of loans, investments, and money they have on hand. Department stores use computers to keep inventory, financial records, and accounts.

Computer simulations are used in many professions. For instance, simulations of flight conditions are used to train airline pilots. Theoretical administrative situations are used to train business managers to make wise decisions. Even car designs are simulated on computers.

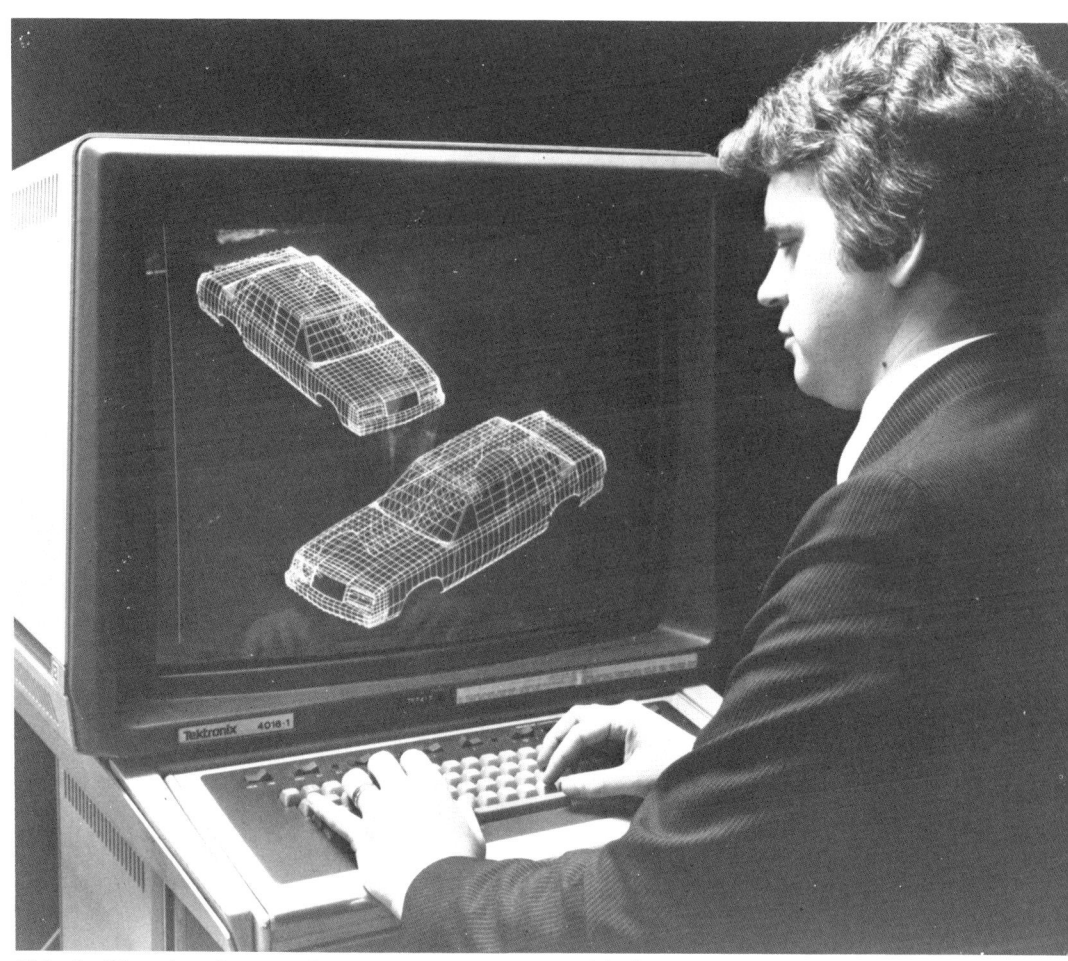

This is Chrysler Corporation's CAD (Computer-Aided-Design) system used to create body designs for 1983 cars.

Chrysler CAD/CAM—Computer-Aided-Design/Computer-Aided-Manufacturing—locates welding sections on vehicles being assembled.

Below, robots run by computers do the welding.

Simulation is effective for training people in areas where actual experience is too dangerous, expensive, or impractical.

Governments are the largest users of computers for tax records, social security information, budgeting and accounting, and many other purposes. Law enforcement agencies place information about criminals, stolen goods and cars, and fingerprints on computers.

Weather data are collected and stored on computers. This information is then used by the computer to make weather forecasts.

The space industry also uses computers extensively. Without computers, the moon landings would have been impossible. Computers were able to do all of the navigational computations rapidly enough to make the space trips possible. If human beings had had to do the computations, we could not have traveled in space for a long time.

The telephone system relies almost totally on computers. In fact, most of the voice messages for number changes or dialing errors are computer-generated.

Schools use computers to keep records and to teach various lessons. Credit bureaus, which keep records on how people pay their bills, use computers to document people's credit ratings.

Can you think of any other ways computers are used?

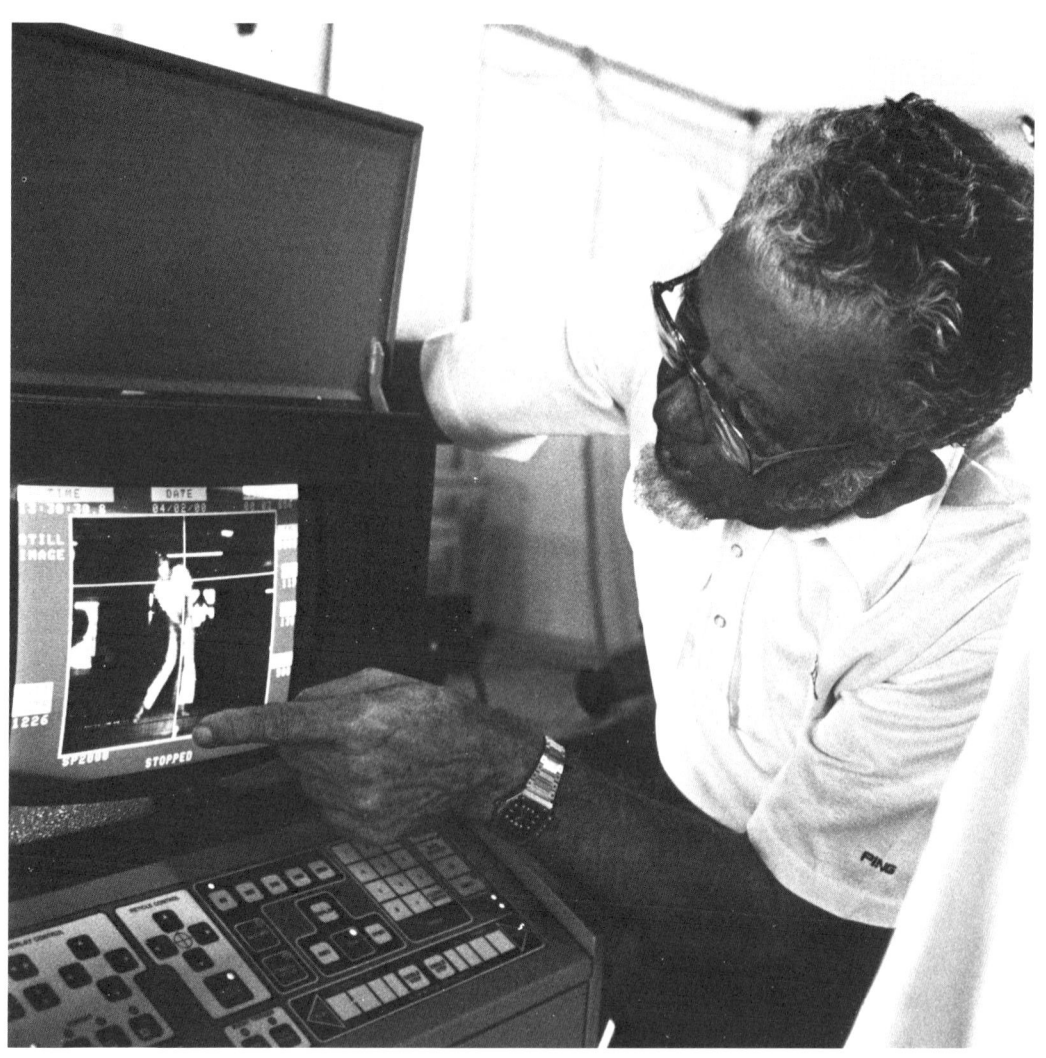

A golf club manufacturer uses computer technology to analyze motions used in playing golf in order to improve their clubs.

The computer is being used increasingly to help the disabled.

Misuses of Computers

Many misuses of computers have been uncovered in the last few years. People have stolen millions of dollars by changing computer programs to help them commit crimes. They have broken computer codes meant to protect information stored in the computer and have had thousands of dollars worth of materials shipped to fake addresses for the purpose of stealing the goods. A fake insurance company used the computer to show accounts and profits it didn't have, so investors would buy its stock for a great deal of money when actually the stock was worth nothing.

The computer's abuse of privacy is a topic that is of concern to many. Concern has been voiced by many groups that too much information kept on computers could be stolen and used illegally or given to people or organizations who should not see it. Safeguards must be developed to protect people against the misuse of private information.

Individuals must also be protected against computer errors. Errors in credit information can cause a computer to deny credit to people who are entitled to it. Often, however, it is hard for people to find out what computer records say about them so they do not know what the problem is and cannot correct it.

Computer Careers

The computer industry has created many new computer-related occupations.

A *systems analyst* examines problems to determine how a computer can be used to solve them. The results go to a *computer programmer* who makes diagrams called *flow charts* of each problem. Then the programmer translates the flow chart into instructions for the computer in its own language—BASIC, FORTRAN, COBOL, etc. A programmer designs and writes programs for the computer and then makes sure that the program runs correctly.

A *systems programmer* writes programs to help organize the many different jobs that the computer must perform.

The *data entry operator* types the programs and data directly into the system on a CRT or teletypewriter. The *computer operator* is responsible for actually working the computer. Both the data entry operator and the computer operator are trained to work with a specific computer.

When the computer system breaks down, the *computer technician* must be called in to make the necessary repairs. In addition to repairing systems that are not working properly, the computer technician also performs routine maintenance checks to keep the system from breaking down in the first place.

Then there are the *computer scientists* who design and develop computers and who think about how computers can and should be used to solve different types of problems. For example, some of these scientists are trying to develop artificial intelligence in a computer. In other words, they are trying to give computers thinking ability.

At the Creative Rapid Learning Center in Austin, Texas, these students are gaining computer skills they can use later in computer careers.

Computers in the Future

Before the turn of the century, most homes will have computers. These computers will be used to control the heating and air conditioning systems in the home, the light switches, and television adjustments. Home computers will keep track of income and expenses, plan menus, and record appointments. Mail will be received and sent by the computer. Libraries and general sources of information will be available through home computers. Education may be carried on in the home instead of in schools when computers are a part of every household. Do you think you would like that? Most financial transactions will be carried out by computers, and we may not need cash at all!

Computer-operated robots, already being used in some factories, will be doing many more jobs.

Computers will be used to diagnose disorders in medical patients. It will be possible to make artificial replacement body parts, such as hearts, controlled by microprocessors. Microprocessor parts may even restore sight, hearing, and speech.

We will also be able to travel in space almost as easily as we now travel in automobiles because of computer-assisted spaceships. And here on the earth, cars will be equipped with microcomputers to warn drivers when maintenance is needed and to diagnose problems.

The future of computers may well be unlimited. We are only beginning our explorations of the computer's capabilities and potentials.

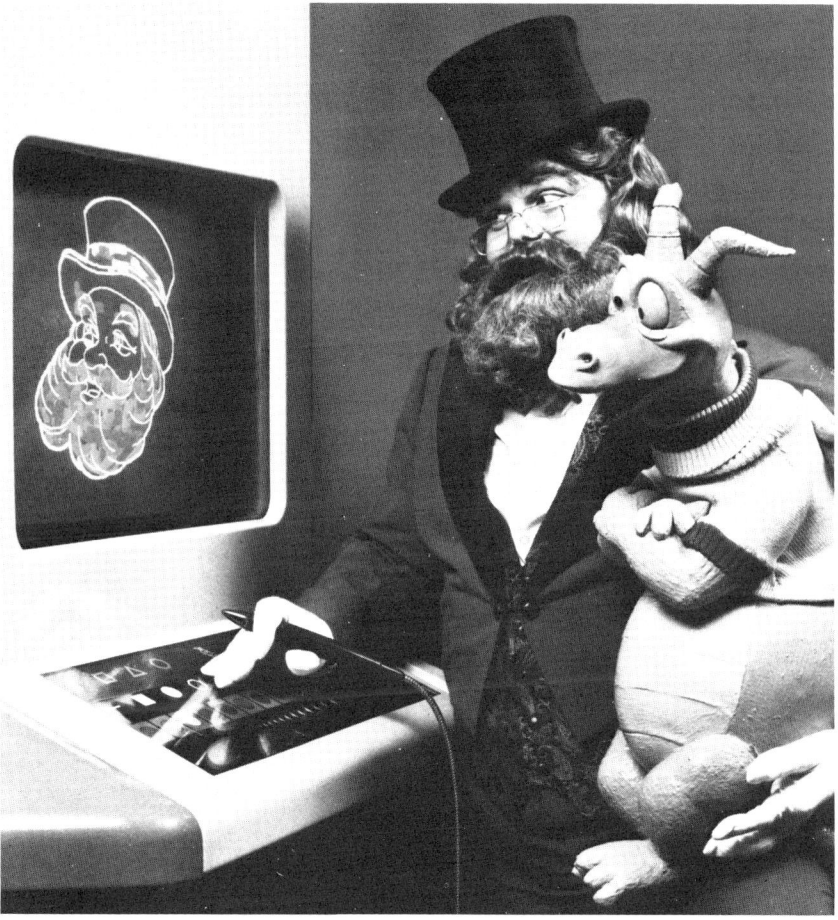

At the Epcot Center in Florida, where technology of the future is on display today, Disney characters Dreamfinder and Figment use the Magic Palette to create computer graphics.

Computer-Related Activities for You

Writing a Flow Chart

Many computer programmers use flow charts to plan their programs. The following flow-charting symbols are used throughout the world.

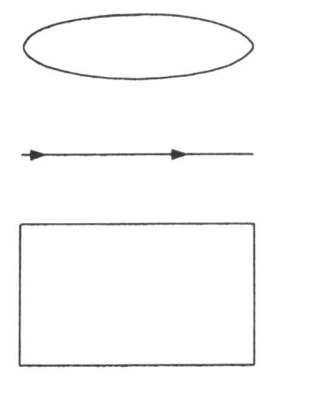

This oval means start or stop.

This arrow tells the direction in which to go.

This rectangle is used for arithmetic or for instructions to be carried out by the computer.

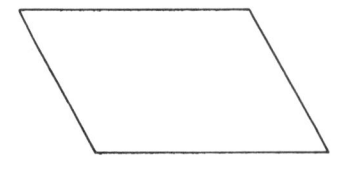

This parallelogram indicates input or output.

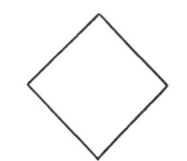

This diamond is used for decisions.

Here is an example of a sample flow chart. Can you figure it out?

This flow chart indicates what some children do when school is out. They walk home and do all their chores. Next, they go out to play. Then they eat, study, and go to bed. Each arrow indicates the step that comes next.

```
START
  ↓
BELL RINGS
  ↓
WALK HOME
  ↓
DO CHORES
  ↓
PLAY
  ↓
EAT
  ↓
STUDY
  ↓
GO TO BED
  ↓
STOP
```

Now let's use all the symbols.
Can you follow this flow chart?

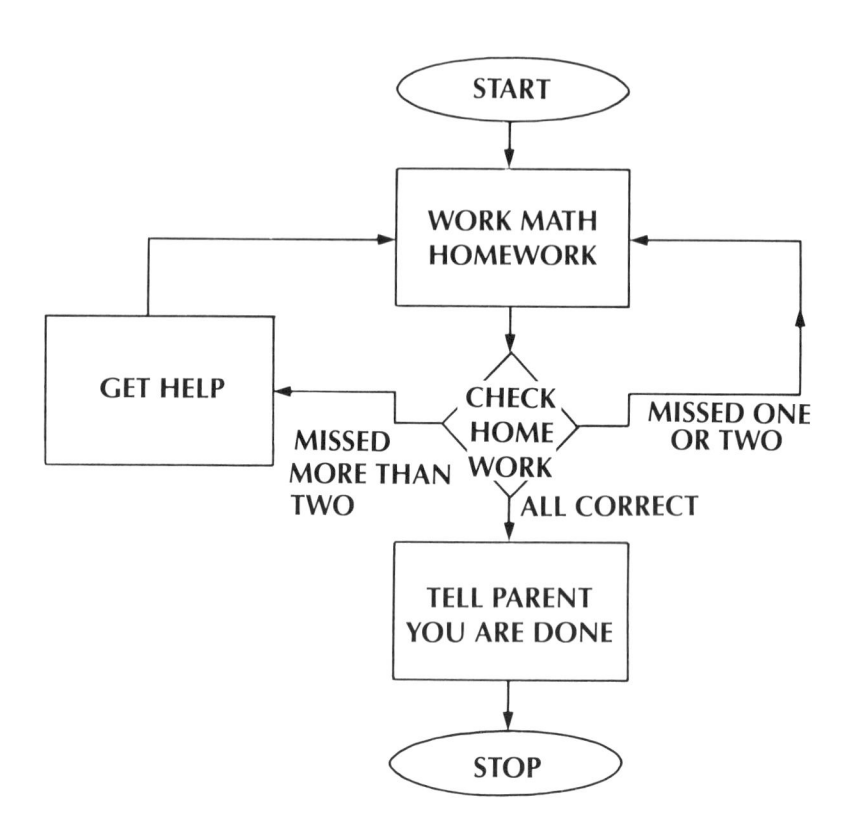

```
                    START
                      │
                      ▼
         ┌──────────────────────┐
    ┌───▶│    WORK MATH         │◀───┐
    │    │    HOMEWORK          │    │
    │    └──────────────────────┘    │
    │                │               │
    │                ▼               │
┌────────┐        ╱CHECK╲    MISSED ONE
│GET HELP│◀──────╱ HOME  ╲──── OR TWO
└────────┘  MISSED╲WORK ╱
          MORE THAN╲   ╱
            TWO     ╲ ╱ ALL CORRECT
                     ▼
         ┌──────────────────────┐
         │   TELL PARENT        │
         │   YOU ARE DONE       │
         └──────────────────────┘
                     │
                     ▼
                   STOP
```

In this flow chart you are to work your math homework. Check the homework. If you missed more than two problems, get help and try again. If and when all your problems are correct, tell your parent or teacher that you are done, and stop.

Thinking Like a Computer

Look at the five cards below. They are named by the number in the upper lefthand corner: the #1 card, the #2 card, and the #4, #8, and #16 cards.

Now ask a friend to think of any number between 0 and 32 without telling you the number. Then have your friend point to the cards that show the secret number. Now add up the card names—2, 4, 8, or 16 of the cards your friend chooses. They will add up to the secret number.

#1 CARD

1	3	5	7
9	11	13	15
17	19	21	23
25	27	29	31

#2 CARD

2	3	6	7
10	11	14	15
18	19	22	23
26	27	30	31

#4 CARD

4	5	6	7
12	13	14	15
20	21	22	23
28	29	30	31

#8 CARD

8	9	10	11
12	13	14	15
24	25	26	27
28	29	30	31

#16 CARD

16	17	18	19
20	21	22	23
24	25	26	27
28	29	30	31

Suppose your friend points to the #1 card, the #8 card, and the #16 card. Add 1, 8, and 16. Your friend's number is 25.

Now suppose the secret number is 14. Where does 14 appear? If 14 is on the #2 card, the #4 card, and the #8 card. The numbers 2, 4, and 8 add up to 14.

Have you figured out how the game works?

The numbers in the upper lefthand corners of the cards—1, 2, 4, 8, 16—are powers of 2. The number 2 to the zero power (2^0) equals 1; 2 to the first power (2^1) equals 2; 2 to the second power (2^2) equals 4; 2 to the third power (2^3) equals 8; 2 to the fourth power (2^4) equals 16. Powers of 2 make up the binary place value system, the same number system that most computers use.

The binary system uses only two digits—0 and 1—in a particular placement to indicate the powers of 2. A computer can register 0 and 1 easily by means of an on-off system: on equals 1; off equals 0. The more on-off switches a computer has, the more capability it has for processing numbers, and those numbers are all powers of 2.

Name the numbers shown by the switched-on lights in the chart on the facing page.

Computer Number Chart

Computer Number   **Our Number**

|	Binary Place Value			
16	8	4	2	1
○	○	○	○	○
●	●	○	●	●
●	○	○	●	○
●	●	●	○	○
●	○	●	●	●
●	○	○	○	○
○	●	●	●	●
●	○	○	●	●
○	○	○	○	○

16 + 8 + 1 = 25

4

8 + 4 + 1 = 13

Number is _____

Number is _____

Number is _____

Number is _____

Number is _____

Number is _____

67

Reading a Computer Program

One of the most common computer languages is BASIC. BASIC stands for Beginner's All-Purpose Symbolic Instruction Code. It was developed in the early 1960s at Dartmouth College.

A computer programmer writes programs like these sample BASIC programs to tell the computer what to do:

These numbers are called program line numbers. They are for computer memory use. Any increasing sequence of digits can be used. If the programmer wants to add anything, he or she can insert it in the proper place by using a program line number between the two numbers where the material should appear. The computer will print out in the proper numerical sequence.

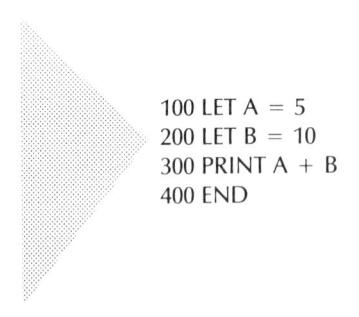

```
100 LET A = 5
200 LET B = 10
300 PRINT A + B
400 END
```

Can you tell what this program will do?
It will add 5 and 10 and print the answer 15.

Try this one:

```
10 LET R = 10
20 LET S = 100
30 LET T = 1000
40 PRINT R, S, T, R + S, T − S, T + S + R
50 PRINT "MY NAME IS GARY."
60 END
```

What is the output of this program?
The output of this program is:

    10   100   1000   110   900   1110
    MY NAME IS GARY.

In this program, line 10 has the computer store 10 in memory location R. Line 20 places 100 in memory location S. And line 30 places 1000 in memory location T.

    Then it is told to print R, which is 10; S, which is 100; T, which is 1000; R + S which is 100 + 10 or 110; T − S, which is 1000 − 100, or 900; and finally T + S + R, or 1000 + 100 + 10, or 1110.

    Next, the computer is told to print "MY NAME IS GARY."

    Line 60 tells the computer that this program is ended.

Program the Mechanical Person

A mechanical person is sitting on a chair, facing a wall a short distance away. Draw the flow chart of the procedure necessary to make the mechanical person walk to the wall and return to its original position. A counter on the mechanical person will add the steps it takes.

The mechanical person only knows these commands:

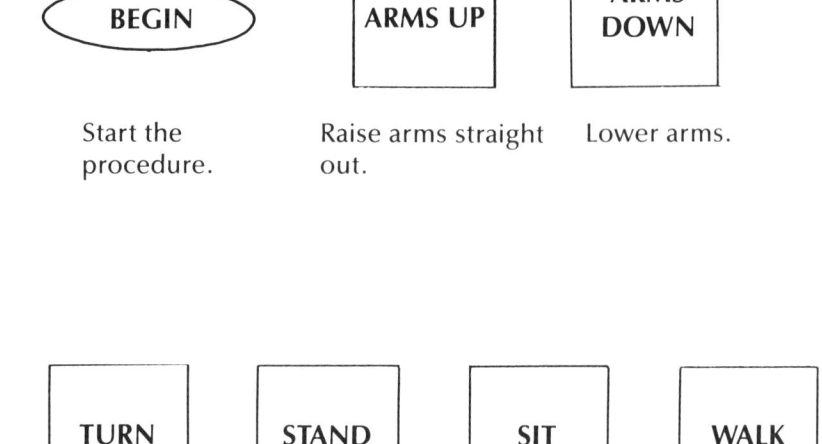

BEGIN
Start the procedure.

ARMS UP
Raise arms straight out.

ARMS DOWN
Lower arms.

TURN
Turn 90° to the right.

STAND
Stand up.

SIT
Sit down.

WALK
Take one step.

70

ZERO	ZERO → NO
Set the counter at zero.	↓ YES Test if counter is at zero.

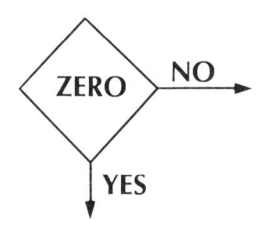

ADD ONE	SUBTRACT ONE
Add one to the counter.	Subtract one from the counter.

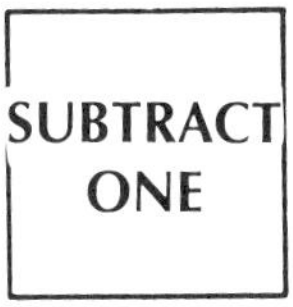

Test for touching wall. Arms must be straight forward to activate the finger control units.

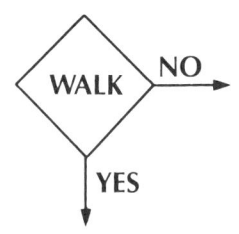

WALK → NO
↓ YES

HALT

Stop the procedure.

The flow chart on the next page will direct the mechanical person to get up, walk to the wall, touch the wall, and return to the seat it started from.

This flow chart would need to be written in a language the mechanical person could understand. With this program, the mechanical person could get up from a chair facing the wall, touch the wall, and return to its seat. Each activity you want the mechanical person to do would need to be programmed into its computer.

Adapted from "The Mechanical Man" by Ken Lebeiko. Reprinted with the permission of Creative Computing, *POB 798-M, Morristown, N.J. 07960.*

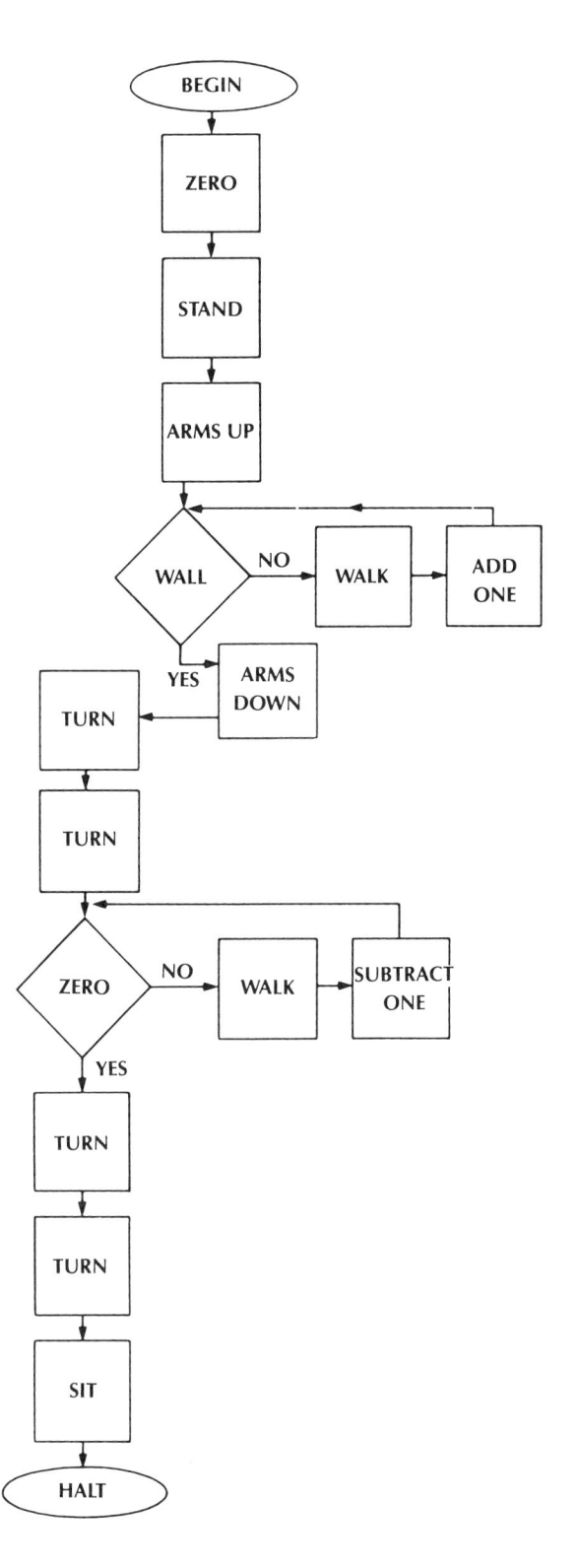

```
                    BEGIN
                      │
                      ▼
                  ┌───────┐
                  │ ZERO  │
                  └───────┘
                      │
                      ▼
                  ┌───────┐
                  │ STAND │
                  └───────┘
                      │
                      ▼
                  ┌────────┐
                  │ARMS UP │
                  └────────┘
                      │
          ┌───────────┴───────────────────────┐
          ▼                                   │
        ╱WALL╲   NO    ┌──────┐    ┌──────┐   │
        ╲    ╱────────▶│ WALK │───▶│ ADD  │───┘
          │            └──────┘    │ ONE  │
          │ YES                    └──────┘
          ▼
     ┌────────┐    ┌───────┐
     │  TURN  │◀───│ ARMS  │
     └────────┘    │ DOWN  │
          │        └───────┘
          ▼
     ┌────────┐
     │  TURN  │
     └────────┘
          │
          ▼                                   │
        ╱ZERO╲   NO    ┌──────┐   ┌──────────┐│
        ╲    ╱────────▶│ WALK │──▶│ SUBTRACT │┘
          │            └──────┘   │   ONE    │
          │ YES                   └──────────┘
          ▼
     ┌────────┐
     │  TURN  │
     └────────┘
          │
          ▼
     ┌────────┐
     │  TURN  │
     └────────┘
          │
          ▼
     ┌────────┐
     │  SIT   │
     └────────┘
          │
          ▼
        HALT
```

73

Computer Graphics

Did you know that you can draw with a computer? Thousands of shapes can be stored in a computer's memory banks. The shapes are printed out on a grid, and the process is called *computer graphics*. A computer program gives the code that calls up the proper shapes and a pair of numbers that says where on the grid to place the shape, using a dot on the shape as an anchor point.

Here is a program adapted from *MATH* magazine.

Program Line Numbers	Code Numbers	Ordered Pairs of Numbers
10	R8	(10, 4)
20	D3	(7, 1)

How many steps are in your program? The program line number of the first step calls up the first shape, R8. Look for R8 on the grid. Is the shape you find a rectangle? Do you see the dot, the anchor point for placement on the grid? That anchor point is placed on the grid where the paired numbers meet: the first number is the horizontal (—) line; the second number is the vertical (|). The first shape, R8, is placed so the anchor point is on the crossing point of lines 10 and 4.

75

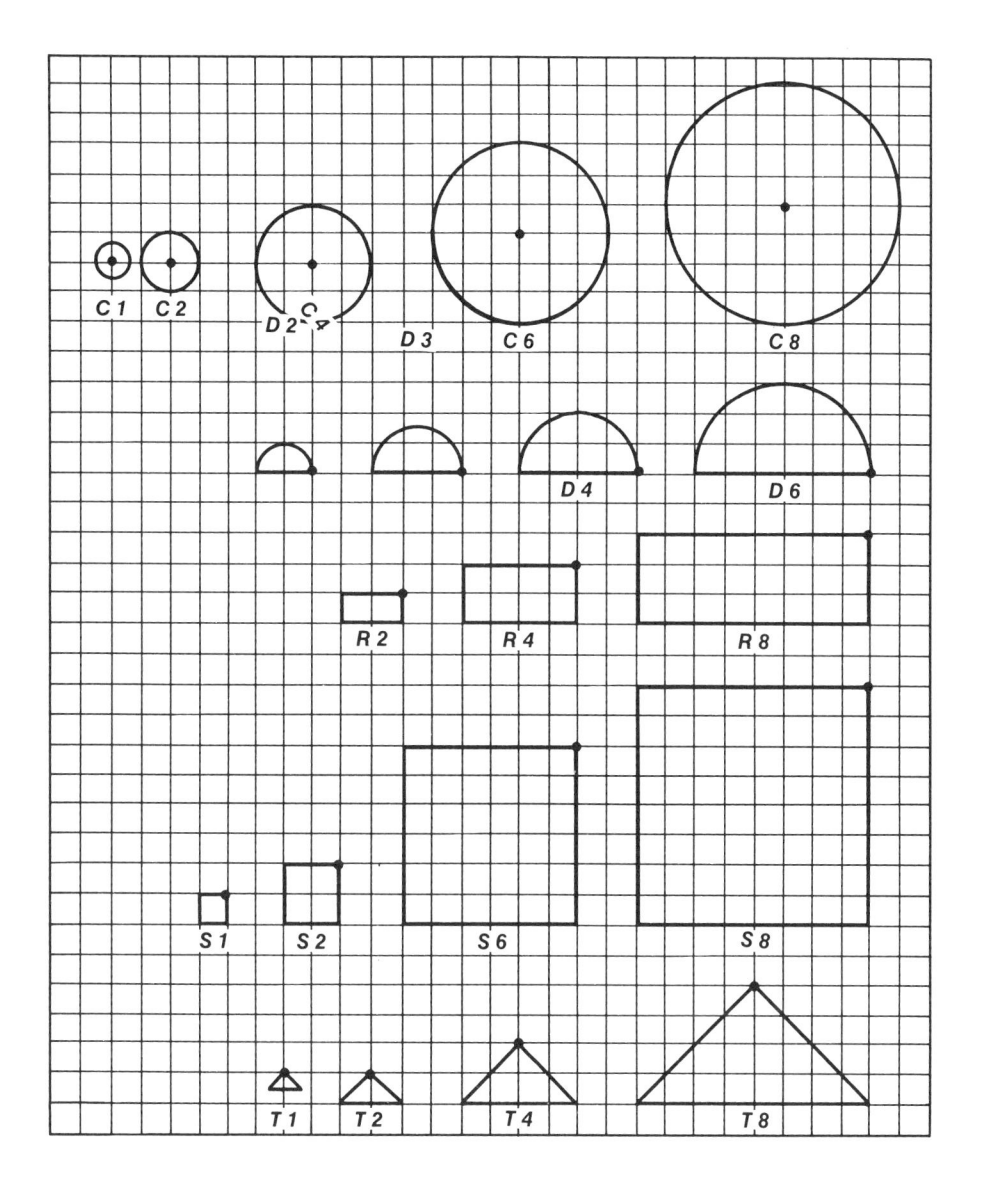

Now go to the second step, program line 20. Your code number will give you the second shape you need. The ordered pair of numbers will tell you where to place it on the grid. Did you get a semicircle? Now you have your picture—a picture of Kojak walking by a high window!

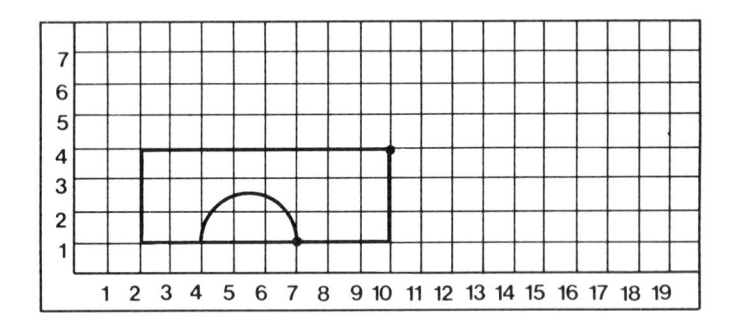

Trace the shapes on the grid in this book, and, using graph paper, work out a picture and program for your own computer graphics.

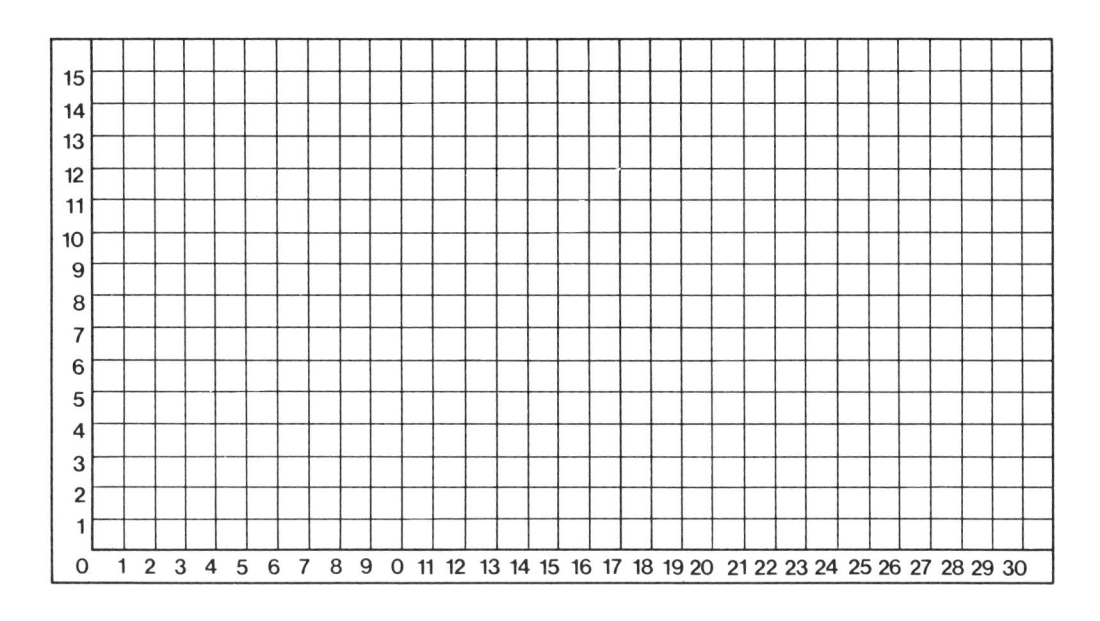

Computer Literacy Questionnaire

Ask several people—adults and children—what they think about computers. Record the results.

	Agree	Disagree	Don't Know
1. Computers are human.			
2. Computers can speak.			
3. Computers hate people.			
4. I would like to own a computer.			
5. Computers are all-powerful.			
6. Computers make few mistakes.			
7. Computers are frightening.			
8. Computers are expensive.			
9. Computers can think.			
10. I like computers.			

How many Agrees do you have for each statement? Disagrees? Don't Knows? Do the results agree with your feelings about computers? What do you think about your findings? Do you think people understand computers? What other conclusions are you able to drawn from your findings?

The Keyboard

In 1872 Christopher Sholes invented the typewriter keyboard. It is usually referred to as the "QWERTY Keyboard," and it is the basis of most microcomputer keyboards.

Why is it called the QWERTY Keyboard?
Why did Sholes arrange the keys in this way?
Do you know other keyboard designs?

Design a keyboard that you think would be easier to use.

The "QWERTY Keyboard."

LOGO

LOGO is a new computer language available for many microcomputers. One application of LOGO is to direct a character, usually called a "turtle," on the screen to make designs. This is often called "turtle graphics."

Here are just a few commands the turtle understands:

FORWARD 10   The turtle will move forward 10 turtle steps.
RIGHT 90   The turtle will turn right 90°.

What will FORWARD 60 have the turtle do?
What will RIGHT 120 have the turtle do?
What shape will these commands have the turtle draw?

RIGHT 90
FORWARD 50
RIGHT 90
FORWARD 50
RIGHT 90
FORWARD 50
RIGHT 90
FORWARD 50

Did you come up with a square?
Write a list of commands to make the turtle draw a triangle.

Is this what you wrote?

> FORWARD 80
> RIGHT 120
> FORWARD 80
> RIGHT 120
> FORWARD 80

Computer Word Find

Find all the computer-related words, abbreviations, or names that have been used in this book. Turn the page for the answers.

```
E X P L O R I N G W I T H C O M P U T E R S
R N Q L B C E K C H N G F E T O A N B A N O
L S I K L M B C O A P J L S U R S I A Z M F
U R R A Z D C R M I U H A N C L C V V Y A T
B A S I C O U T P U T D N B O A A A Q P I W
I V O K I T H Z U O N G I P K N L C B L N A
N M N E R R A M T S V P M M W D X Z D C F R
A E P N C G F E E I J A R I H A R D W A R E
R B A B U J R M R V T S E C S M D A Y I A Q
Y X R M I C R O E L E C T R O N I C S B M Z
X K L K T T E R U W M A D O P J S U C R E W
Y V I Q S S L Y L V F L N W E X K M R O Q A
C E N T R A L P R O C E S S I N G U N I T R
```

81

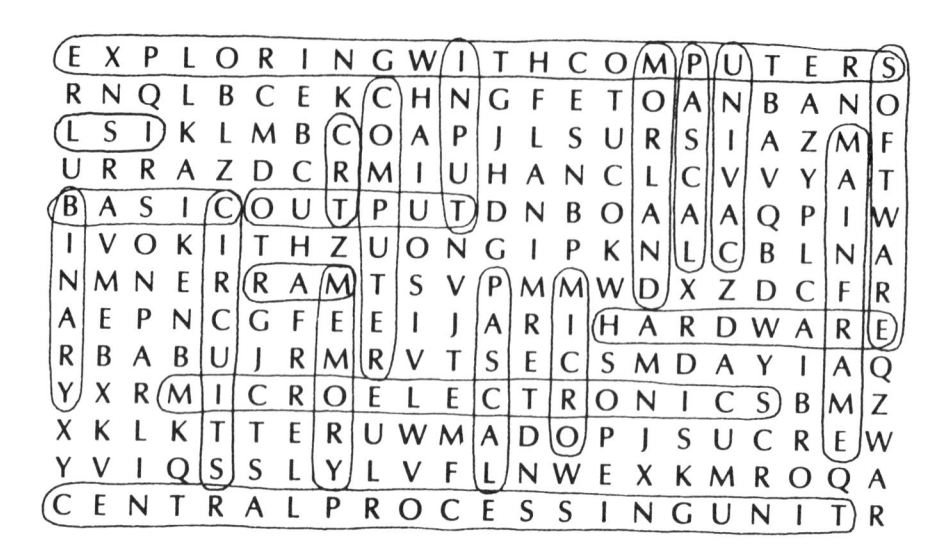

E	X	P	L	O	R	I	N	G	W	I	T	H	C	O	M	P	U	T	E	R	S
R	N	Q	L	B	C	E	K	C	H	N	G	F	E	T	O	A	N	B	A	N	O
L	S	I	K	L	M	B	C	O	A	P	J	L	S	U	R	S	I	A	Z	Y	F
U	R	R	A	Z	D	C	R	M	I	U	H	A	N	C	L	C	V	V	P	M	T
B	A	S	I	C	O	U	T	P	U	T	D	N	B	O	A	A	A	Q	P	A	W
I	V	O	K	I	T	H	Z	U	O	N	G	I	P	K	N	L	C	B	L	I	A
N	M	N	E	R	A	M	T	S	V	P	M	M	W	D	X	Z	D	C	F	N	R
A	E	P	N	C	G	F	E	E	I	J	A	R	I	C	H	A	R	D	W	A	R	E
R	B	A	B	U	J	R	M	R	V	T	S	E	C	S	M	D	A	Y	I	A	Q
Y	X	R	M	I	C	R	O	E	L	E	C	T	R	O	N	I	C	S	B	M	Z
X	K	L	K	T	T	E	R	U	W	M	A	D	O	P	J	S	U	C	R	E	W
Y	V	I	Q	S	S	L	Y	L	V	F	L	N	W	E	X	K	M	R	O	Q	A
C	E	N	T	R	A	L	P	R	O	C	E	S	S	I	N	G	U	N	I	T	R

Glossary

Abacus: an instrument used for recording numbers by sliding counters (usually beads) along rods or grooves.
Atanasoff, John Vincent: designed the ATANASOFF-BERRY computer in 1930s with student Charles Berry but not recognized until 1970s.
Aiken, Howard: outlined a plan for a digital computer in 1937.
Applications software: instructions that tell a computer how to solve a particular problem.
Arithmetic/Logic unit: the part of the computer that performs computations.

Babbage, Charles: invented the "analytical engine" in 1834.
BASIC: Beginner's All-Purpose Symbolic Instruction Code. A widely used computer programming language.
Berry: see **Atanasoff.**

Bit: Binary digit.
Byte: set of bits, typically eight, the smallest unit in computer memory. Each letter of the alphabet can be represented as a byte. *see also* **Kilobyte.**

Card reader: a machine that "reads" information from punch cards and sends the information to the computer's central processing unit.
Cathode Ray Tube: CRT. A televisionlike screen that shows information as it is entered into the computer.
Central Processing Unit: CPU. Controls the input, output, memory, and arithmetic/logic units of the computer.
Chip: a unit of large-scale integrated circuits.
COBOL: Common Business-Oriented Language. A computer programming language used primarily in business.
Computer operator: a person who actually works the computer.
Computer programmer: a person who writes the instructions that tell a computer what to do.
Computer scientist: a person who designs and develops computers or thinks about how computers can and should be used to solve different kinds of problems.
Computer technician: a person who maintains and repairs computer hardware.
Computer terminal: a machine with a keyboard like a typewriter used for entering information into a computer.

Data cards: See **punch cards.**
Data entry operator: a person who enters information into the computer.

Eckert, John Presper: led a project with John William Mauchly that developed a computer called ENIAC between 1943 and 1946.
EDVAC: Electronic Discrete Variable Automatic Computer. The first computer to store a set of directions.
Electro-mechanical switches: mechanical switches controlled by electricity.
ENIAC: Electronic Numerical Integrator and Computer. A large, vacuum-tube computer built between 1943 and 1946.

First-generation computers: vacuum-tube computers developed between 1945 and 1959.
Flow chart: a diagram used by computer programmers to show the different steps in a program.
FORTRAN: Formula Translator. A computer programming language used mainly by scientists and engineers.
Fourth-generation computers: large scale (LSI) and very large scale (VLSI) integrated circuit computers developed since 1975.

Hard-copy terminal: a paper printer that shows information as it is entered into the computer.
Hardware: the equipment that makes up the computer system.
Hollerith, Herman: used punch cards to "program" a calculating machine in 1887.

Input: the process of entering information into a computer.
Integrated circuit: a small, single unit containing numerous electronic components of a computer. Also called microelectronics.

Jacquard, J. M.: used punch cards to produce designs in cloth woven on looms.

K: See **kilobyte.**
Keypunch: the process of using cards punched in coded patterns to perform computations.
Keypunch operator: See **data entry operator.**
Kilobyte: 1,024 bytes or units of information.

Large Scale Integration: LSI. The process of reducing many circuits into one unit (chip).
Lovelace, Lady: assisted Charles Babbage in his work on the "analytical engine."

Magnetic core: a form of primary storage.
Magnetic disk: a form of secondary storage.
Magnetic tape: a form of secondary storage.
Mainframe: the largest type of computer system.
MARK I: a huge electro-mechanical computer built in 1944.
Mauchly, John William: led a project with John Presper Eckert that developed a computer called ENIAC between 1943 and 1946.
Microcomputer: a relatively small-sized computer system. Also called a home computer or a personal computer.
Microelectronics: see **integrated circuit.**
Microprocessor: a CPU contained on a single chip, designed to perform a specific job.
Minicomputer: a medium-sized computer system.
Morland, Samuel: invented a mechanical calculator in 1662.

Output: information the computer comes up with after performing computations.

Pascal: a computer programming language named after Blaise Pascal.
Pascal, Blaise: invented a calculating machine in 1642.
Place-value number system: a system of numbering in which the position of a digit determines how much the digit represents.
Primary storage: memory capacity inside the computer.

Punch cards: cards with holes that represent a special code that the computer understands.

Random Access Memory: RAM. Memory that can be changed at any time, unlike ROM.
Read Only Memory: ROM. Stored instructions built into the computer for repeated use.

Second-generation computers: transistorized computers developed between 1959 and 1964.
Secondary storage: memory capacity outside the computer.
Semiconductor memory: the main memory of a computer.
Simulation: using the computer to create conditions similar to real experiences.
Software: the set of instructions or programs given to the computer to tell it how to work.
Solid state amplifiers: see **transistors**.
Systems analyst: a person who examines problems and decides how a computer can be used to solve these problems.
Systems programmer: a computer programmer who designs programs to organize different jobs performed by the computer.
Systems software: instructions that help control and schedule the parts of the computer system.

Teletypewriter: a paper printer that shows information as it is entered into the computer.

Third-generation computers: integrated-circuit computers developed between 1964 and 1975.

Time-sharing: a system in which several people or groups share the use of a single computer system.

Transistors: replaced vacuum tubes in computer technology during the second generation of computers. Also called **solid state amplifiers**.

UNIVAC I: the first commercial computer, developed in 1951.

von Liebniz, Gottfried Wilhelm: invented a calculator in 1694 that could multiply and divide as well as add and subtract.

von Neumann, John: used binary arithmetic in developing high-speed computers, including EDVAC.

Index

A
abacus, 12
ADA, 16
Aiken, Howard, 18
airlines, 38
"analytical engine," 16
applications software, 40
Arithmetic/Logic unit, 28-29, 33.
 See also Central Processing Unit
artificial body parts, 60
artificial intelligence, 27, 28
Atanasoff, John Vincent, 18
Atomic Energy Commission, U.S., 21

B
Babbage, Charles, 16
banking, 37-38, 44, 50

BASIC, 40, 68-69
Berry, Clifford, 18
binary arithmetic, 21
Byron, Augusta Ada, Lady Lovelace, 16

C
card reader, 30
Cathode Ray Tube (CRT), 30, 37-38, 41, 58
census, U.S., 17
Central Processing Unit (CPU), 28-29, 32, 36, 41
chip, 24-26
Chrysler Corporation, 51, 52
COBOL, 40, 41
coding, 30-31

computers, powers of, 11; as a tool, 11; history, 12-27; digital, 18; MARK I, 18; ATANASOFF-BERRY, 18; ENIAC, 19, first-generation, 19; EDVAC, 21; UNIVAC I, 21; transistors in (solid-state), 22; second generation, 22; integrated circuitry (microelectronics) 22; LSI, 24; VLSI, 25; third generation, 23; fourth-generation, 25-26; future, 27, 60-61; industries and, 37-38, 44, 50-52; languages, 16, 40-41; users of, 44-55; in government, 17, 44, 53; careers, 57-59; in medicine, 60
computer graphics, 61, 74-77
computer languages, 16, 40-41, 57. See also named languages
computer literacy, 78
computer operator, 58
computer scientists, 58
computer technicians, 58
computer terminal, 30
control unit. See Central Processing Unit.
CPU. See Central Processing Unit.
CRT. See Cathode Ray Tube

D

data entry operator, 58
Department of Defense, U.S., 44
disk, magnetic, 36, 41

E

Eckert, John Presper, 18
electro-mechanical switches, 18
Epcot Center (Disney World, Florida), 61

F

flow charts, 57, 62-64, 72-73
Forth, 40
FORTRAN, 40, 41

H

hard-copy terminals (teletypewriters), 30, 37, 58
hardware, 40, 41
Harvard University, 18
Hewlett-Packard Corp., 26
Hollerith, Dr. Herman, 17
home computers. See microcomputer

I

input, 28-29, 30-31.
integrated circuitry (microelectronics), 22, 23
International Business Machines (IBM), 18, 26

J

Jacquard, J. M., 16

K
keypunch, 30
Kilby, Jack, 23
kilobyte (K), 33-34

L
Large Scale Integration (LSI), 24
LOGO, 40, 41, 80

M
mainframe computer systems, 44
Mauchly, John William, 18
memory, computer, 28-29, 32, 33; primary, 33-35; secondary, 36; RAM (Random Access Memory) 34; ROM (Read Only Memory) 34; semiconductor, 34; magnetic core, 34; magnetic tape, 36; magnetic disk, 36
microelectronics. *See* integrated circuitry.
microcomputers, 46, 60-61
minicomputer systems, 44
misuse, computer, 56-57
Morland, Samuel, 15

N
number systems, Roman and Hindu-Arabic, 12-13; place-value, 13

O
odometers, 13
output, 28-29, 37-39

P
Pascal (software language), 40
Pascal, Blaise, 13
privacy, abuse of. *See* misuse, computer
programmers, computer, 57; systems, 58
punch (data) cards, 30

Q
QWERTY keyboard, 79

R
robots, 60

S
schools and computers, 44, 46, 53, 60
Sholtes, Christopher, 79
simulations, computer, 50-53
software, 16, 40-41
solid state amplifiers, 22
space travel, 53, 60-61
storage. *See* memory
systems analyst, 57
systems software. *See* software

93

T
tape, magnetic, 37
telephone systems, 53
teletypewriters. *See* hard-copy terminals
Texas Instruments, 48
time-sharing, 44
transistors, 22

"turtle graphics." *See* LOGO

V
vacuum tubes, 19
Very Large Scale Integration (VLSI), 25
von Leibniz, Gottfried Wilhelm, 15
von Neumann, John, 21